William Bolcom

Suite
for
Violin and Violoncello

in Five Movements

Prelude - Very free and fast
With energy
Stately, slow
Very fast and skittish
Street dances

World Premiere: Sergiu Luca and Roel Dieltiens
Brussels, Belgium, November 17, 1997

EDWARD B. MARKS MUSIC COMPANY / HAL•LEONARD® CORPORATION

EXCLUSIVELY DISTRIBUTED BY

7777 W. BLUEMOUND RD. P.O. BOX 13819 MILWAUKEE, WI 53213

for Sergiu Luca and Roel Dieltiens

Suite for Violin and Violoncello

WILLIAM BOLCOM
(1997)

Duration: 12:00

1. Prelude

Very free and fast (♩ = 80 ←→ 90, molto rubato at times)

* hard-pulled - **not** snapped

NB: Accidentals obtain only throughout a beamed group.

8/6/97

2. With energy

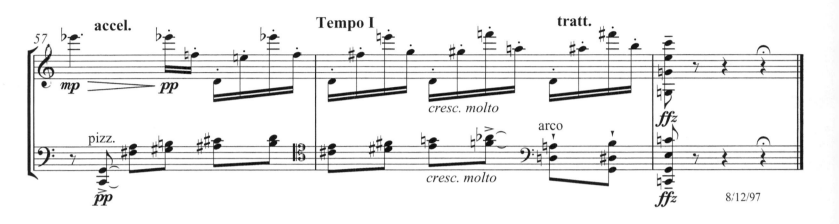

8/12/97

3. Stately, slow

8/22/97

4. Very fast and skittish

8/23/97

5. Street Dances

♩ = 84 or slower
rhythmic, in strict time

* Noteheads with an x are fingered with the thumb of the left hand.

8/29/97
Ann Arbor